*"Everything begins with mysticism,
and ends with politics."*

Charles Péguy

Forthcoming from Robert Davies Publishing :

The Traitor and the Jew : antisemitism and the echos of fascism among the extreme right-wing nationalist elites in Quebec from 1929 to 1939, by Esther Delisle

Editorial assistant : Madeleine Hébert

Please address any enquiries to :
Robert Davies Publishing, c/o
Stewart House, 481 University Avenue, Suite 900
Toronto, Ontario M5G 2E9L

Pierre Elliott Trudeau's historic speech
at the eleventh Cité libre dinner

Trudeau :
"A mess that deserves a big
NO"

Translated By George Tombs

ROBERT DAVIES PUBLISHING

DISTRIBUTED IN CANADA BY

**Stewart House, 481 University Avenue, Suite 900
Toronto, Ontario M5G 2E9
☎ (Ontario & Quebec) 1-800-268-5707
(rest of Canada) 1-800-268-5742
Fax 416-940-3642**

ISBN 2-89019-250-4

1 2 3 4 5 6 7   1992 1993 1994 1995 1996

A note from the publisher

ON THE SECOND THURSDAY OF EACH MONTH, *Cité libre* welcomes its readers and friends for good food and lively discussion at the now-famous Maison Egg Roll, a Chinese restaurant in the working-class Montreal district of St-Henri. In the sixteen months since the magazine began to publish after a long hiatus, the speakers have included Jacques Renaud, Albert Breton, Jacques Henripen, d'Iberville Fortier, Ovide Mercredi, Esther Delisle, Jean-Louis Gagnon, Jean-Claude Leclerc, Gérard Pelletier, and Charles Taylor, with the subjects debated ranging fromFree Trade and the Post-Modern world to Individual Freedom and Right-Wing Nationalism in the Quebec of the 1930s.

October 1, 1992 was an especially memorable evening for *Cité libre*. Four hundred guests in the room were joined by a half-million Quebeckers listening in live on the Quebec Telemedia radio network, while millions more in the rest of Canada held their breath to hear what the guest speaker was going to say about the Charlottetown Accord and the referendum debate. Their patience was soon rewarded, as the readers of this book will discover in page after page of verbatim transcript of the speech, the debate, and a high-voltage press conference held immediately afterwards. More than one hundred members of the fourth estate huddled in a separate room of the restaurant, grumbling about the no-camera, no-TV, no-press rules in the main hall. But the sound was piped in, so they could listen, snack on expense-account Moo Goo Guy Pan and prepare their questions for the speaker's first full press conference in eight years. Trucks sporting twelve-foot satellite up-link dishes ringed the restaurant, national television news personalities arrived early in the afternoon to

«Why didn't you hold the dinner at the Ritz?» inquired the news chief of one of the networks. «You could have had a thousand paying guests at a hundred bucks a plate!». He was sharply told off by Anne-Marie Bourdhouxhe, the magazine's editor-in-chief. *Cité libre* is a magazine open to anyone who uses their brains for critical thinking. Having the funds for an glitzy dinner is not a major priority of this magazine.

After the buffet, the hall became completely still as the speaker rose and rang in the tone of his speeach with a sobering quotation from Victor Hugo. In less than forty minutes, speaking without notes but with a copy of the Concensus in hand, he had delivered a stinging attack on the Consensus, calling it a «crippling blow to the Canada we know and love». In newsrooms across the country runners flashed the signs to the men and women already on the air. It's NO, they said. It's NO.

A man who some current politicans had naïvely called «a voice from the past» had, like Pythagoras, shown that critical thought never goes out of fashion. It was, for the current crop a leaders, an unhappy game of political fifty-two pick-up.

Some in the Maison Egg Roll agreed with the speaker's analysis, and some dissented. That is what *Cité libre* is all about. Their is no set political line in a magazine of free thought and speech. But every person who spoke with passion and reason had in mind the future of this great land. Whatever your own position, whether you agree or agree to disagree, you owe it to yourself to read the words of the guest speaker at the eleventh *Cité libre* dinner, October 1, 1992.

Robert Davies

Introduction

GOOD EVENING, LADIES AND GENTLEMEN, and welcome to the Maison Egg Roll in St. Henri and the eleventh monthly dinner of *Cité libre!* My name is George Tombs and I am your MC this evening. Of course, MC does not mean 'maître chanteur' [master blackmailer], as those people who have read Mr. Trudeau's article in *L'actualité* [and *Maclean's*] can well imagine. MC stands for master of ceremonies. I could have asked all those in favour of YES to sit at my right, and those in favour of NO to sit at my left. But that would have created a lot of problems, since there isn't enough space in the kitchen for undecided voters. Anyway, I will be along shortly to give a hand washing the dishes.

Clearly, this evening is not just any evening. First of all, the timing. We are in the middle of a referendum campaign which fills some people with dark anxiety, not forgetting that it fills all the others with dark anxiety as well. In any case, that's what our politicians and bankers are telling us. And then, there's the fact that we have managed to attract not just two hundred people to our dinner, the way we did when Ovide Mercredi was our guest, but four hundred people. Which beats all our attendance records. And besides, thanks to CKAC-AM and the Télémedia radio network, we have something like a half million listeners around the province, tuning in to the thirty stations of the Télémedia network.

Just because this is the first time we have had so many people listening to us, whether on their walkman, in taxis, at home or at work - that's a lot of people - I'd like everyone here this evening in St. Henri to extend a warm welcome to our listeners throughout the province. (Applause.)

Perhaps I should say a few words about *Cité libre*, the magazine *Cité libre*. The first version of the magazine was founded in the 1950s by Pierre Elliott Trudeau and Gérard Pelletier. After an absence of many years, the magazine resurfaced again a year ago: its guiding principle is that freedom and diversity of opinion are at the very foundation of an open and democratic society. It's clear that the people who have built the *Cité libre* team are a group of young, dynamic and very independently-minded people. I'd just like to present to you our publisher, Anne-Marie Bourdouxhe; and that indispensable person who does proofreading and rewrites, Marie Desjardins. OK! I can't name everybody, but I know you'll be getting up later to ask questions. A few members of our editorial board. Stephen Schecter. Is Stephen here tonight? No, OK. Robert Davies... and Louis-Philippe Rochon, who has brought a lot of his students from the University of Ottawa.

In the current issue of the magazine, coming out on newstands this week, some of our contributors express their viewpoints on the referendum. Six have come out in favour of the YES side, including myself, with two against, and one abstention which seems to have turned into a NO in the meantime. So the magazine has not taken a unified editorial position, we have no line to follow, except that we believe Quebec and Canada are compatible, and we can work things out, get along and build a better country for the future.

At *Cité libre* we have a tradition - I'll just keep you waiting another minute or two - we have a tradition of inviting a distinguished person to speak to us about an important topic. After which, our guest discusses the topic openly with the rest of us, during a period of questions and answers, or remarks and replies.

I want to remind you that the evening takes place in French. And so, for our anglophone friends, who don't speak French very well - that is, if there are still anglophones who can't speak French! - I won't say the way they do in some Montreal churches: 'For our English-speaking friends, your contributions are appreciated, especially in the collection plate!' You are welcome, and I invite you to participate in the way that suits you best. But since the magazine is a French-language magazine, we would appreciate it if you made the effort to speak good French, if you please. I'm going to have to limit the questions to one or two minutes - roughly, eh - and as for any journalists sitting in on our dinner, I would just ask you to give a chance to the citizens to speak. Because it isn't every day that, shall we say, 'ordinary' citizens are able to pay $20.00 for a good meal and the opportunity to talk about the future of the country with a former Prime Minister of Canada. And lastly, since CKAC and the Télémedia network are broadcasting the evening across the province, I would ask everyone to identify themselves when they reach the microphone, and to make their question clear. And could everyone else please keep quiet, nicely, so everything runs smoothly.

Now, without more ado, our guest. No doubt you have all read Mr. Trudeau's article in L'actualité. An article which left nobody indifferent. I don't have to tell you that Mr. Trudeau does not often have the chance to speak directly to Canadians, without passing through the filter of the media. If he has agreed to speak to us this evening, it is because he doubtless has things to say / I still don't know what exactly, I am not aware of that /but above all because he, Mr. Trudeau, wants at this moment in time to have a real discussion, back and forth, with his fellow citizens. Ladies and Gentlemen, without keeping you waiting any longer, I have the honour of presenting to you the Right Honorable Pierre Elliot Trudeau.

Speech of the Right Honourable
Pierre Elliott Trudeau

Good people, beware of the things you say!
Anything can emerge
From a word you let drop in passing,
Anything, hatred and mourning.
And do not protest that you can trust your friends
and that you speak softly.
Listen carefully to this.

WELL, THIS QUATRAIN FROM VICTOR HUGO is to let you know that the word you let drop in passing, when you vote, the YES or the NO, is very important: so important that you cannot simply base the word you choose on emotions, or on what Anne-Marie Bourdouxhe, in the editorial of the current issue [of *Cité libre*] describes as anxiety, fear or impatience. We will have to use some reason, some analysis. Because it is no small matter to know whether we are going to live in a society in which personal rights, individual rights, take precedence over collective rights. It is no minor question of secondary importance to know whether we are going to live in a society in which all citizens are equal before the law and before the State itself. And it is no trivial matter to determine if there will be a spirit of brotherhood and of sharing in the society we are going to live in.

The choice we are going to make in the referendum, the choice of which society we want, has an impact on these three questions. And to know what choice to make, we have to look at the texts. I am not trying to say that those people who give preference to a collective society and collective rights over individual rights, do not have the right to state such a preference. I am saying to them that it is not just an emotional decision they are called on to make. We have to look at history - above all we have to look at contemporary history, the history of yesterday and today.

When collective rights take precedence over individual freedoms - as we see in countries where ideology shapes the collectivity, where race, ethnic origin, language, and religion shape the collectivity - we see what can happen to the people who claim to live freely in such societies. When each citizen is not equal to all other citizens in the state, we are faced with a dictatorship, which arranges citizens in a hierarchy according to their beliefs. And when a person lives under the reign of unbridled capitalism, it is not sharing and justice that prevail, but rather the law of supply and demand. The implacable market decides how wealth is distributed.

So we must reflect on these questions. And to be in a position to reflect, I will have to read you some of the main items of the text which is called 'the Consensus of Charlottetown', the text on which citizens are asked to vote YES or NO. Unfortunately, high-level politicians and even high-level bankers want us to believe that voting YES is 'a yes to Canada' while

NO is 'a no to Canada'. This is a lie that must be exposed.

The question 'yes or no' is just that: yes or no, do you want to reform, do you want to amend the Constitution of Canada on the basis of the so-called 'Consensus of Charlottetown'. So let's take a look at it.

Don't worry, I don't intend to go into too much detail. I imagine that whoever wanted to have a copy of the report has been able to obtain one. So I won't read out all the items: far from it!

I will start with the Canada Clause, the first one telling us that 'the Constitution of Canada, including the Charter of Rights and Freedoms, shall be interpreted in a manner consistent with the following fundamental characteristics'. Which means that when judges come to judge the validity or invalidity of a citizen's challenge of a law of a province or of the federal government which undermines his freedoms and constitutional rights, the judges will have to rely on this Canada Clause. Well then, I submit to you that this Canada Clause offers us a hierarchy, a hierarchy of categories of citizens. We are not equals according to this Canada Clause. It all depends on where each individual stands. And I will name the six categories in which the eight or ten sections of the clause place you, the citizens. You will have to decide where your place is in that hierarchy.

I will start with category number one, the first and most important one, the clause referred to as 2.1c):

'Quebec constitutes within Canada a distinct society, which includes a French-speaking majority, a unique culture and a civil law tradition.' And, significantly, they add that 'the role of the legislature and Government of Quebec is to preserve and protect the distinct society'.

In other words, in interpreting any case which comes before them, judges will have to bear in mind that in the province of Quebec, the government has the right to apply laws, the legislature has the right to pass laws, which will promote the unique culture of Quebec, and that the Charter of Rights and Freedoms must be interpreted taking this fact into account. It is not surprising that the cultural communities [an expression denoting Quebec's so-called ethnic minorities] who are not Quebeckers of old stock, are worried: they are not a part of this unique culture, they are much lower down among the categories of the Charter. It also means that the Charter of Rights and Freedoms, currently enshrined in the Constitution, must be subject to interpretation taking into consideration the francophone majority. Collective rights, as voted into law by the majority in the National Assembly of Quebec, must guide judges in their interpretation of the Charter of Rights and Freedoms and, in fact, of the Constitution in its entirety.

Second category: 'the Aboriginal peoples of Canada ... have the right to promote their languages, cultures and traditions ... and their governments constitute one of three orders of government in Canada.' They will have governments, and legislatures, but it isn't made clear, we haven't seen the texts, but the Charlottetown Charter announces this news!

First of all, these governments are granted the right to invoke the notwithstanding clause, to invalidate the sections of the Charter which otherwise would protect individuals. I refer you to section 2, and item 43 [of the Canada Clause]. On the subject of Aboriginal peoples, section 2 says: 'nothing in the Charter abrogates or derogates from Aboriginal rights and in particular any rights and freedoms relating to the exercise or protection of their languages, cultures or traditions.' To which item 43 adds, in so many words: 'the legislative bodies of Aboriginal peoples should have access to Section 33', the notwithstanding clause. In other words, they want to give governments and legislatures to Aboriginal people, and they say there are eleven principal native languages in Canada, in addition to forty tribes and six hundred bands. I don't know how many of these units will qualify as governments or legislatures. But in any case, we are forewarned there will be a lot of governments, and, by virtue of the fact they are governments - the item is clear about that - they will have the notwithstanding clause. And it will be practically impossible ever to get rid of this clause, which was included in the 1982 Constitution as the price to pay to obtain a Charter. So forget about seeing the notwithstanding clause disappear!

Third category of citizens. Take note of the first category - 'the *role* of the Government of Quebec is to preserve and promote the distinct society'; the second category - 'Aboriginal peoples *have the right* to promote'; and the third category / 'Canadians and their governments are *committed* to the vitality and development of [official language] minority communities'. A lot of people have noticed this. I won't dwell on it. In English, the text reads 'commitment'. In French it reads 'attachement', which is an emotional impulse, not a 'commitment'. And this 'attachement' will return over and over, whenever it is a question of categories 3 and 4.

Notice that when it comes to *equalization payments*, the translator of the English word 'commitment' suddenly discovers the French word 'engagement' [a solid commitment], because Quebec is solidly committed to equalization. But only the French word 'attachement' is used to refer to the vitality and development of minority communities.

And we can see why: with your permission I will read you clause 1.3. Allow me to disabuse anyone of the notion that this 'commitment' protects minority communities, whether English-speaking in Quebec or French-speaking in Alberta and Saskatchewan. I will read to you the sub-clause, that is, paragraph 3 of clause 1: 'Nothing in this section derogates from the powers, rights or privileges [relating to language] of the legislatures or governments of the provinces.'

So whatever provinces want to give precedence to their prvincial laws, Bill 101 or suchlike, are now given the green light. No wonder there is no more than an 'attachement' to the idea of the development of official language minority communities. Let me also read you item 28 which shows how the doddering fools meeting in Charlottetown considered the question of commitment to minority communities. Item 28 says, on the subject of labour market development and training, that powers should be passed over to the provinces, the way they are for forestry, mining, etc.

And the same phraseology keeps coming back: 'Considerations of service to the public in both official languages should be included in a political accord and be discussed as part of the negotiation of bilateral agreements.' Now there's a strong commitment for you!

They say the same thing in practically the same words for forestry and the other items: 'Considerations of service to the public in both official languages should be considered a possible part of such agreements.' So you can imagine what will happen when federal jurisdictions are handed over to the provinces. The federal government is obliged to offer services to any citizen who requests it in one or the other of the two official languages. Does anyone think this will be maintained in Alberta, in Quebec, or possibly in Manitoba? Well, so much for the third category of citizens.

And now a fourth one. The fourth results from the commitment of Canadians and their governments: 'Canadians are committed to racial and ethnic equality.' First of all, this considerably weakens Section 15 of the Charter. Mentioning that Canadians are committed to racial equality is, I think, a little like saying 'Well, I have some black and Jewish friends, you know, I'm committed to them, but let's not talk about granting them rights.'

Same wording, but it doesn't apply anyway, this 'commitment' when it comes to Aboriginal lands. Let me read you an outrageous item, item 46. [In the French text Mr. Trudeau refers to, item 46 is called 'La participation des non-Autochtones aux gouvernements autochtones' which means literally 'The participation of non-Aboriginals in Aboriginal Governments,' while in the official English version of the text it is called 'Provision for Non-Ethnic Governments']. In other words, unless there are native people here at this meeting, the rest of us, you and I, can only *perhaps* participate in such a Government .

'Self-government agreements may provide for self-government institutions which are open to the participation of all residents in a region covered by the agreement.' I will not insult native people by saying they are the ones who wanted this clearly racist article. Let's just say 'people other than ourselves will be allowed onto our lands'. But the Canada Clause tells us Canadians are committed to racial and ethnic equality!

Same wording in the following article: 'Canadians are committed to a respect for individual rights'... Wouldn't the word 'commitment' *alone* be nice? Oh but wait, I left out a few words: 'Canadians are committed to a respect for individual *and collective human* rights and freedoms'. Oh, I see, they want to please everybody. You, over here, you say you are committed to a society where collective rights are tops? OK. In your neck of the woods, people are 'committed' to collective rights. And you, over there, you prefer that individual rights win out? That's quite all right, we are committed to your individual rights too. But what happens when a contradiction arises? When collective rights run headlong into individual rights as guaranteed by the Charter? How will the courts decide?

Is there any ... we haven't seen the actual text. All we've seen is this *thing* [the Consensus Report]. Apparently, they have written texts. But citizens are not interested in reading the legislative texts, they will have to be satisfied with generalities. Well, generalities.... They tell us, you know, don't worry about it, nobody will have to choose between collective rights and individual rights, since *both* are recognized. Well, really!

Here again, the same kind of commitment, in the following article, the following [part of Section 2 of the Canada Clause]: 'Canadians are committed to the equality of female and male persons.' I hope the ladies are happy to hear that people are committed to the principle of the equality of the two sexes and that the courts will have to weigh the commitment of Canadians to this equality. Not evidently to the extent that it could be at variance with a law created by the upper categories [of our hierarchy], which have *solid commitments* from the government, whereas in your case, you only have an 'attachement'.

By the way, the Canada Clause doesn't even mention that Canadians have a 'commitment' to the Charter of Rights and Freedoms. Because *that* document is another story, with *clear and precise* language.

On the subject of equality, let me read you section 15 of the [existing] Charter:

'Every individual is equal before and under the law and has the right to the equal protection and equal benefit of the law without discrimination and, in particular, without discrimination based on race, national or ethnic origin, colour, religion, sex, age or mental or physical disability.'

That's what we had. But now, the people voting YES will have to say: 'all that will be weakened, because there are new interpretative clauses. Any interpretation of the Constitution, especially of the

Canadian Charter of Rights and Freedoms, will have to agree with the fundamental characteristics.' So what they're in the process of saying to the judges is: if discrimination is based for example on colour, religion or age, the Charter applies; but in the case of the rights of the two sexes and the rights to cultural and racial diversity, Canadians are only *committed*. Which is akin to saying that those kinds of discrimination are less important. So, good-bye!

Well, now we have finished with category 4, and we move on to category 5 in the new hierarchy of rights of Canadian citizens. The fact that Canada is a democracy committed to a parliamentary and federal system, as well as to the rule of law, is a fact. There's no right to *promote*, there's no *commitment*, it's just a *fact*. But this fact is not even binding on Aboriginals, once you look at item 41, which lets them legislate according to their traditions, their culture and all the rest.

And while we're in in the fifth category, how about the fact that 'Canadians confirm the principle of equality of the provinces at the same time as recognizing their diverse characteristics'. That's really something: they confirm the equality of the provinces, after having said in the same article, in a sub-clause, that Quebec is a *distinct* society and it is the *only* distinct province in the Constitution. So what is this now about telling the provinces they are all equal?

Moreover, if you read item 58, you will see other examples of inequality. You will see that new provinces being created do not have the same rights as existing provinces. It's a great idea to create provinces in the Far North, but don't imagine that will automatically give you the right to participate in the Senate on the same basis as the others or to participate in the amending formula. Well, so much for the fifth category...

Now you may ask me where are all the remaining people, all those who do not deserve to be included in this enumeration, all those who have been named in the Charter and who are not named in this Canada Clause. They are bunched together with - what was his name in L'Aiglon [a play by the French author Edmond Rostand, first presented in 1900]? 'And we the little people, the privates, marching footsore'...

Mr. Robert La Palme, from the floor: 'Flambeau'.

Mr. Trudeau: 'Flambeau', thanks! There's a cultured man! As I was saying...: 'And we, the little people, the privates, marching footsore and dirty, hungry, sick'... Well, that's all the rest of you, you are in the sixth category in this Canada Clause.

Let's leave the Canada Clause then, and talk about the ... no, wait a second, it's still the Canada Clause, but it's the third sub-paragraph. A real beauty!

'Nothing in this section derogates from the powers, rights or privileges of the Parliament or the Government of Canada, or of the legislatures or
governments of the provinces, or of the legislative bodies or governments of the Aboriginal peoples of Canada, including any powers relating to language'. So it
doesn't undermine the powers of any government.
Whose power is it supposed to undermine? 'The rest
of us, the little people, marching footsore and dirty!'
So, now it's clear that everyone is really protected from
... the Charter! The Canada Clause does not undermine the rights of all our politicians, it only undermines ourselves, as I have just explained to you, by
diminishing the power of the Charter. It's either a dis-
grace, or something bordering on sheer stupidity, for
them to state this so openly.

Well, let's move on to another clause. They talk
of 'social and economic union'. OK, the social and economic union. Let's just summarize it by saying that article 4 is not enforceable, which means that they use
great-sounding words, but it does not have the force of
law. Much the same for the Canadian common market. They talk about a political agreement no-one has
seen, and of future conferences, but this common market, which was the only thing the Canadian government was asking for in this 'Canada round', does not
even appear in the final text, where there is only room
for the provinces and the Aboriginals. Nothing for you,

nothing for Canada! So get lost, if you are interested in making the common market a fact!

We now move on to federal institutions ... The Senate is elected ... *but it can be elected by provincial legislatures*, they already said that's the way Quebec would be appointing Senators. Which means literally that a provincial government can come between its citizens and the Parliament of Canada when it legislates in areas of federal jurisdiction. So not only do they give powers to the provinces, but in addition, they say: you can sit in the Senate and pass laws with us. That wouldn't be true if the Senators were elected, but it remains true when they are appointed by a provincial legislature: it is always the majority, that is, the government that determines what people will say. That's what their Senate *reform* amounts to.

Laws materially affecting [French] language or culture have to be adopted by a double majority of francophone Senators taking part in the vote. Imagine the case of a separatist government in Quebec which has not yet made Quebec independent, but which names its Senators. It will presumably send six Senators to Ottawa, in addition to which there will perhaps be other francophone Senators from other provinces, but the ones from Quebec have a veto. So, we will need the vote of a majority of Senators for a law to pass, which means that if ever the Government of Canada wants to improve the status of francophones in the West or, God forbid! the anglophone minority of

Quebec ... well, the separatists can use the veto. And it's not inconceivable. After all, we know that Quebec, Mr. Bourassa's *federalist* Quebec in fact, went to Alberta and Saskatchewan to plead against the francophones from those two provinces who were trying to get their rights recognized by their provincial Governments. Quebec pleaded in those provinces because they didn't want English-speaking Quebeckers to be able to say: *we want the same thing.* Its incredible, the lengths to which the narrow-mindedness of Quebec nationalism will go.

The Supreme Court ... The judges will be named on the basis of lists submitted by the provincial governments. That's a guarantee that the cause of the provinces will always win out over the cause of Canada itself. The provinces will name the judges of the Supreme Court, they will - once the Supreme Court is completely renewed - it will only consist of judges named by the provinces. And inevitably, the provinces will not name die-hard federalists, they will name people in line with their own views. And according to what we see here, because the ten provinces have signed this charter, or at least they haven't signed it yet but they have adopted it, they favour massive decentralizaton. Which means the judges will always hand down judgments in favour of the provinces. Of course, this could have an unforeseen boomerang effect, because the other provinces may start wanting more for themselves and be ready to give less to Quebec. Quebec only has three judges, the other provinces have six. What a mess it will be to have the three judges of Quebec always lining up on one side and the six on the other; people will cry out at the 'injustice'... after having created this mess themselves!

House of Commons ... Given the time left to me, I won't talk about that.

Entering the First Ministers Conference into the Constitution. Well, it will always be ten against one as soon as you start deciding things in a Conference which has become a constitutional *obligation*.

Roles and responsibilities: that was the last point I wanted to raise. There's lots to say about that, but let me just say that this group of clauses on roles and responsibilities comes down to one thing: the federal government is to cede jurisdictions to the provinces. I am not saying that if the provinces had a top-notch record in applying their present exclusive jurisdictions everywhere.... Take education, for example. Quebec has control over education, and has had exclusive and complete control over education ever since the beginning of Confederation... Well, Quebec has the highest high-school drop-out rate in the Western world. I read that myself in L'actualité[the newsmagazine] a few months ago. The highest dropout rate: it's not the fault of les *Anglais*, it's not the fault of the *federal* government, it's *our* fault. Fifty percent of students graduating from high school fail their French entrance exam at Laval University. That's not the fault of *les*

Anglais! Forty percent of high school students fail the entrance exams at the Université de Montreal! Who was it that prepared them for these exams? Was it *communists?* Or did we do that ourselves?

Take a look at the environment ... or just a minute, look at culture, at libraries for example. Ontario has four times more libraries than Quebec, taking into account the size of their respective populations. They spend *four times as much* in Ontario as in Quebec so that the people can read.

Look at the environment, like sewage treatment systems for example. Ninety-five percent of cities and towns in Ontario have them, but only thirty-three percent in Quebec. And now these people would like to obtain *new* powers, while in fact they are doing a poor job of exercising the powers they already have. So, this whole section is really just a power grab! Let's go on to federal spending power. Well then, if this particular article becomes law, you can forget about new national programmes to help out the smaller or poorer provinces, because there will always be a right to opt out if it's a national programme. Provincial governments will be able to say: 'if I already have a compatible programme, I am opting out, and you, Ottawa are going to compensate me for it'. Inevitably, all the rich provinces will expect compensation. But no federal politician will vote for the rich provinces getting all that money! And so there won't be any for the poor provinces either.

People always want to limit *federal* power to spend. But they neatly forget that the provinces make abundant use of their *own* spending power. Have you ever wondered how it is the province of Quebec and the province of Ontario and the province of Alberta have diplomatic missions abroad? Do they have jurisdiction over foreign policy? Is that somewhere in the Constitution?

Or again, when they give money to African countries, to promote Quebec on the international scene, where do they get that money? From your taxes! *That's* spending power. The provinces never complain about *their* spending power, sometimes they even use it to give bursaries or to help francophones from other provinces in the case of Quebec, and it's the same thing for anglophone institutions who come to the assistance of Quebec anglophones. That's spending power. But now, they don't want the federal government to have spending power, so there will no longer be any *shameful* programmes like health insurance or hospitalization insurance: let's not have things like that! Let's instead give money to the provinces so that they remain unequal : the poorer provinces will have less-well funded programs, which will be the case with Quebec, and the rich provinces will be able to get the best of everything!

And on it goes... Immigration. '[A new provision should be added to the Constitution] committing the Government of Canada to negotiate agreements with the provinces relating to immigration.' There are no limits on the provision, they talk of no limits. At least with Meech Lake there were some limits, but here there are none. So that means there there will no longer be a national immigration policy. All the provinces wanting their own policy will get one.

Same thing for the labour market, same thing for culture. It's true that provinces, when it comes to culture ... what is culture? ... you'll see how they defend these demands. Quebec doctors, apparently, when they do an appendicitis operation, they don't do it the same way as in Ontario? They have a special culture? And does the the same goes for haircuts? Well! The provinces want to have exclusive *jurisdiction* over cultural questions on their territory, but the federal government would continue to have *responsibilities*. I don't know whether words *mean* anything here, but the federal government would have *responsibilities* without having *jurisdiction*, because the provinces would have jurisdiction. This probably means that the federal government would pay money, enjoying *responsibilities*, while the provinces would actually have constitutional jurisdiction here.

Forestry, mining, tourism.... Canada will be the only country in the world unable to do promotion itself abroad for tourism. Sounds great? Housing... forget about federal money going into low-income housing. Recreation... it isn't defined either. Does this mean all the national parks in Canada, where people pursue recreational activities, all of that is going to be provincial? Nobody knows. Do you know what recreation is? No, I don't know either. We have recreational activities, but when they say in the Constitution that recreation is entirely a provincial jurisdiction, I have a lot of trouble with that.

Municipal affairs. OK, article 92 already lays that out. But what's all this about urban affairs? Does this mean there will no longer be any federal presence in the development of large cities? And yet, the federal government is railways, the post office, and I don't know how many investments in infrastructure, in federal buildings for example. The federal government will no longer have a word to say, when it comes to the development of cities.

(Mr. Trudeau, aside to Mr. Tombs: 'I know you stole ten minutes from me: don't get impatient!')

I'm coming to the end, to the end. Yes. I'll stop here. Except that I would like to draw a conclusion.

Those people who plan to vote YES, because they are fed up with constitutional discussions, because they want to finish with it all, or because they are afraid of the instability of banks, just let me say a few words to them. This document is not an agreement. I will read you what it is. I am looking at the preface, on page ii. They tell us that in the course of discussions, draft constitutional texts have been developed whenever possible. In particular, a rolling draft of legal text for Aboriginal peoples.

They don't want to show us those texts! They want us to judge on the basis of the texts I have here this evening. And yet they say that there are areas where the consensus was not unanimous. These dissents have been recorded in the chronological records of the meetings but not in this summary document. So, it's a *consensus*...with some dissension.

But then they add: the asterisks. There are twenty-six asterisks in the text that follows to indicate the areas where the consensus is to proceed with a political accord. So you think you will have finished with the Constitution by voting YES! You will have twenty-six asterisks to resolve, without counting all the other unresolved issues, without counting the dissensions, and the six hundred Indian bands who will want to negotiate. You think you will have peace and quiet by voting YES! You will have peace and quiet if you vote NO, because NO means we are fed up with the Constitutional debate, and we don't want to hear about it any more.

Let me tell you something else. If you think we have finished, think about what Mr. Bourassa said two or three days ago: 'a YES vote is not irreversible, because the negotiations will continue, because we maintain our right of self-determination'. So the people who are voting YES to have peace and quiet evidently haven't listened to what Mr. Bourassa is saying, or to what Mr. Rémillard is saying. They may be listening to what the other Prime Minister is saying, but they have not listened to Mr. Bourassa. He is going to be back asking for more, that's what he is saying. The Allaire Report hasn't disappeared, it's still part of the Liberal Party platform, it has only been set aside for the time being. And the right of self-determination is still in the programme of the Liberal Party of Quebec. What does that all mean? It means the blackmail will continue if you vote YES.

I will make one last comment. If you vote YES, and the YES wins out, the decision will be *irreversible*. It is not like the pendulum of Confederation, which sometimes swings towards centralization and sometimes towards decentralization. The decision is irreversible. First of all because the veto will apply to the Senate, to the House of Commons, and to the Supreme Court. We will not be able to do anything with these institutions any more, without the consent of all the provinces. And as far as jurisdictions are concerned, whatever has been transferred to the provinces - recreation, culture, all of that, even with a constitutional amendment it will be impossible to take it back from the provinces: because there is a lot of compensation for provinces refusing to give up powers they already have. So it will be irreversible.

And moreover, the sad fact is the federal government will have thrown overboard all its advantages, its bargaining power, because the federal government is left with very few advantages. Ottawa still had the power of disallowance and reservation, and the declaratory power. But in this contract [the Charlottetown Accord] it gives that up. And the federal government will be stripped naked if the YES side wins, it will never go after the notwithstanding clause, it will never go after the common market, it will have nothing to give in exchange.

So don't ask me how I am going to vote. But let me will tell you that if you want peace and quiet, you should vote NO to constitutional negotiations. The problem of Aboriginal peoples can be resolved in the legislatures. And once things have settled down, we can talk about how to put that in the Constitution. For the time being, they have made a mess, and this mess deserves a big NO. Thank you very much.

QUESTION PERIOD

Mr. Tombs: We are now opening the floor to discussion, to the people in the restaurant here this evening. Please try to keep your questions from getting too, too long. The first question goes to Dr. Kimon Valaskakis. Until recently, Kimon was vice-president of the board of directors of *Cité libre*.

Kimon Valaskakis: Mr. Trudeau, just as you always do, you have offered us [this evening] a very rigorous and persuasive analysis of the weaknesses of this agreement, which is not the sort of agreement likely to win a management award from the Harvard Business School. We all agree on that. But I would like to take your analysis a step further, and place it in context to suggest that voting NO will make the things you fear actually get worse. There are two aspects to this context. First of all, while we in Canada discuss how many seats the Senate is going to have, what the distinct society is all about, and what the Canada Clause amounts to, four hundred thousand jobs have been lost. Between June and December 1991, we lost a thousand jobs per day, and these lost jobs have created a lot of suffering, which, according to some observers, is due to the conflictual relations between the eleven governments. So I agree that the conflictual relations between the eleven governments, the balkanizing of

Canada is very negative. But won't this balkanizing continue, won't it worsen, with a NO vote?

And that is where the second aspect comes in. I think we find ourselves in a worldwide dynamic nowadays of centrifugal versus centripetal forces. We saw that with Maastricht. We saw how, in France, there was a coalition on the NO side which had nothing to do with Maastricht. And I submit to you, Mr. Trudeau, that we have here [in Canada] a very, very heterogeneous coalition on the NO side.

If I was convinced that voting NO meant voting for all the reasons you have given, I would be tempted to follow your example. But I think that what will happen, when all is said and done, is that people will forget the *Cité libre* dinner tonight, they will forget the arguments, and what will leave its mark on history is that the NO side will have won, that the *nationalists* will have won, and that the centrifugal forces will become greater and greater. And at that point, if we have another constitutional round, won't the situation worsen? You know that at Meech Lake, there were eleven people around the table. At the Charlottetown meeting, they had become seventeen. In the next round, couldn't we be faced with twenty-four or twenty-five, where every group would want to defend its interests? In other words, doesn't the dynamic compel us to choose the lesser evil, in order to put an end to this infernal cycle of centrifugal forces?

So much for my remarks. The question I would like to ask you, Mr. Trudeau, is why, when you speak out with such eloquence in debates, as you spoke out in the case of Meech, and now you have spoken out again in this debate ... Why have you not spoken earlier on, in order to influence the debate, and propose a vision for the 1990s, the way you proposed a vision for the 1960s, and which gave us the means to win the 1980 referendum? Thank you.

Mr. Trudeau: Maybe you should have recommended to the Beaudoin-Dobbie Commission, that they invite me, or maybe to the Bélanger-Campeau Commission, or to the Spicer Commission? Why didn't you ask them to invite me? I wasn't invited...

Mr. Valaskakis: Do you need an invitation?

Mr. Trudeau: Yes, yes, of course I do! I was invited by *Cité libre* here tonight. Listen. I have known you as an intellectual, Kimon, and it seems to me that in those days, you pushed your thinking right to the limits, you were looking for the truth, the best truth, the best solution. *Now*, you are in politics, you have given us a purely strategic, a purely tactical argument. You didn't tell me anything about substance. You admitted it's rotten, it's bad, it's indefensible, well at least you didn't say the opposite, but you are saying what do you want us to do, there's unemployment. Well, who caused all this unemployment?

Mr. Valaskakis: Do you accept the lesser evil, do you accept the argument of the lesser evil?

Mr. Trudeau: Yes, but this evil is worse, it is the *greater* evil to trap yourself irremediably in a Constitution which will destroy the Canada we know, a Canada of equality for all without distinction. Here [in the accord], they are weakening the Charter of Rights. That's what the text says.... the talk I've just given. Now, in the name of tactics... Well, I respect politicians. Perhaps I should change my tone. I respect the people who are voting YES. As George said, there are four, six of them writing in *Cité libre*, maybe more.

(Mr. Tombs: I am not a politician, eh?)

Mr. Trudeau: No, no. Let's say a ... speaker! I understand people are anxious, but it's not my role to hold them by the hand and say 'calm down'. If bankers want to scare us, then don't be scared. But bankers themselves: how much do they earn, Kimon - you're an economist - when the exchange rate goes up two points like that? How much money does that make for the banks? But the bankers can say what they want. Just tell us how much they make, Kimon, our economist, when the exchange rate goes up by two points?

Mr. Valaskakis: Excuse me, but it isn't the companies and the banks that frighten me.

Mr. Trudeau: Oh no, so it's not them?

Mr. Valaskakis: It's the unemployed, 400,000 unemployed.

Mr. Trudeau: Isn't it the bankers who are telling us we need stability, and if you don't vote YES, that will create instability? When a banker says it creates instability, and there's a chance people will vote NO, isn't the banker himself a bit responsible for the consequences? And maybe also the people in the government who don't tell us anything about the substance of the text but who tell us 'you know we have to finish with separatism'. But that's not the *question* they have asked us; they asked us whether we want this particular agreement or consensus. So, we replying to *that* question, and then they tell us 'you see, there is instability in the country!' Who created this instability? Who has been running the economy for the last eight, ten years: it's Mr. Bourassa, Mr. Mulroney. It's not me, I've been out of the picture for a long time. So if there's unemployment, don't let them tell you that you have to do as the government says and go and blindly vote for a lousy accord. If Mr. Mulroney is unable to resolve the situation and the unemployment he has created, then he should just resign. We will find somebody else!

Mr. Tombs: We will move on to the next question. Louis-Philippe Rochon.

Louis-Philippe Rochon: In the current issue of Cité libre, I wrote an article called 'Zut' ['Damn!'] My reasoning was as follows: the accord, the agreement makes me feel sick to my stomach. I put it that way, but I recognized or I feared the consequences of a NO vote. So I said, should I vote YES in spite of my convictions, or should I vote NO in spite of my fears? In the last three weeks, I have completely changed my mind: I have gone over to the NO side, period. You have just spent thirty, thirty-five, forty minutes explaining to us the Canada Clause, article by article, and referring to the other clauses of the agreement, in spite of the fact our politicians in power are saying Canadians will not look at the clause. Maybe they take us for a bunch of fools, I don't know. But how can we explain that the federal politicians, Mr. Mulroney and even Mr. Chrétien, are repeating to us that a NO vote means [Quebec] independence and the end of Canada? Why?

Mr. Trudeau: Go ask them! Listen, go ask them! But I haven't heard Mr. Chrétien say that a NO vote meant the end of Canada. Mr. Mulroney maybe, but I haven't heard Mr. Chrétien say that. No, Mr. Chrétien is a little like my friend Kimon: he is in politics, and I respect the decisions politicians make because they are caught between a rock and a hard place, and they don't know how to get out of that situation. But when you're not in politics, when you don't have obligations, when you are free, free of all partisanship, I think you have to take your thinking to the limits, otherwise we end up bending the truth. Leave that for the politicians! As for the rest of you, you have definite ideas and the right to express them.

Mr. Tombs: OK, the next question goes to the former associate editor of *Cité libre*, Angéline Fournier.

Angéline Fournier: I hope, Mr. Trudeau, that you are not implying people in politics are incapable of independent thought. I am going to tell you something. I am going to vote YES on October 26th, and for the following reason: I belong to a generation, the young generation, which has only known constitutional strife: we have been sacrificed for a constitutional ideal, and the Canada and Quebec we know is a free-for-all. So here, for once, whether we like it or not, is an agreement, a consensus arrived at by democratic means with the First Ministers and the Aboriginal people. What you are doing, is taking the agreement out of its political context, taking it apart piece by piece, and you have done that brilliantly, and I agree with some of your points. And then you say, 'therefore you should vote NO'. Well let me tell you that you are putting dynamite under the bridge, and when the bridge blows up, there will be nothing to replace it with. I don't think it is at all alarmist to say that. It's just that we want to build a future, we are fed up with hearing the East and West of Canada can't get along, and Quebec doesn't belong in Canada, and Canada has nothing to offer Quebec. And I understand something else: if the independantistes campaign for the NO side to create chaos, I can see how that's in their interest. But that people like you and some others who still believe that Canada and Quebec cannot live without each other should push for a NO vote, even when we know full well, and you don't need a crystal ball to see it, that the end-result will be another free-for-all. It's something I just don't understand, and I think it's an intellectual luxury which we, in the current state of Canada, cannot afford. So let me tell you, let me suggest that all these energies we have, these creative energies, should be used to build the future, to develop a vision for society which can really exist and allow us to get on with our lives. So... Let me ask one very short little question: for young people like me who believe Quebec and Canada can't do without each other, what's going to happen the day after a NO vote? And I would like you to give me a concrete answer, and not just something divorced from reality.

Mr. Trudeau: You are asking me to join you in the building of a vision for society, but right here [pointing to the document of the Charlottetown Consensus] you have the vision for society. That's the one you want for Canada? Because there is a consensus, but is among the premiers of the provinces, who were all dishonestly making power-grabs for themselves. And by the way, it's only normal, considering that the federal bar was open, that they should go have a drink. The federal government offered just about anything, and so they took it. Of course the ten provincial premiers want more power for themselves, but what is hard to understand is why the federal government should be ready to give up everything and ask for nothing in exchange. And I understand even less, why people like you, who want peace and quiet for yourselves and your descendants, why you are ready to live in a society where collective rights take precedence over individual rights, in a society in which citizens are arranged in a hierarchy and where the Charter of Rights does not make everybody equal. I find that amazing. And in the name of I don't know what sort of imaginary peace, by the way, because you are really dreaming if you think the separatists, the so-called federalist nationalists, will ever stop asking for more. They will continue asking for more. You hope to have peace? Well, the way to make peace with someone who is constantly blackmailing you is to say NO! It isn't to say YES because then, they will continue blackmailing you.

Mme. Fournier: But the mistake we have been making for the last ten years is to believe that a vision for society is the same thing as a Constitution. That's what I want to say, so I am stepping away from the microphone, but it's not just a Constitution.

Mr. Trudeau: The Consensus Report on the Constitution, that's what the documents pretends to be. But the Constitution is not just a newspaper you buy and then rip up the next day. A Constitution is a vision for society, as you said so well, so it's a society in which people want to live, I hope at least for a generation or two. It isn't a bargain you make like in a union contract, a collective agreement which is good for one year and then after that you go back and ask for ten cents or a dollar more. If that's the way you see things, that's also the way Quebec nationalists see it: they will take everything they can get now, and then a year or a month from now, they will ask for more. If that's your vision for society, well it sure isn't mine. A vision for society is when you say: fine, we are all adults, we are in a democracy, you there in Quebec, you the nationalists, you Mr. Allaire, you Mr. Bourassa, tell us what you are going to want for the next twenty years, for a generation. It's no exaggeration to think of a Constitution lasting one generation. Tell us what you want for twenty years, and have the leader of the Opposition tell us as well, because in the parliamentary system we alternate, right? So go and agree on what is the maximum you want; then we'll decide, and that will be our vision for society for twenty years to come. We aren't going to hold a referendum every ten years on independence. Tell us what will satisfy you for let's say a generation and a half, thirty years. And if that's too much to ask of you, well then 'OK boys, beat it, go make a country on your own, we in Canada are going to continue without you'. Or, if they can handle it, fine, we'll have peace for twenty years. Let's get serious here. When you put together a Constitution, a vision for society as you say, at a given moment people should be able to agree and say OK.

Mr. Tombs: Michel Simard.

Michel Simard: Good evening, my name is Michel Simard. Mr. Trudeau, I listened to your explanations, as well as your remarks. My question will be brief. Should I conclude that you personally would have preferred, as a Canadian, as a French-Canadian living in Quebec, after the Bélanger-Campeau report came out, after the big round of ultimately provincialist speeches we all heard in Quebec and elsewhere in Canada, should I conclude you would have preferred a precise question asking 'Do you want Quebec to become a new country?'

Mr. Trudeau: I think if we aren't able to say what we want, in a clear way, for one generation or thirty

years as I just said; if we want to continue using nationalism for blackmail and say each time there is a new
Allaire Commission or a new Bélanger-Campeau
Commission that we are able to get more powers in
order to dismantle Canada; if we aren't able to say
that's the limit and we won't go farther; if we aren't
able to say Mr. Bourassa was wrong and didn't mean
what he said, when he said a YES is reversible or that
you can say YES to this package but don't worry because we still have the clause on self-determination,
and tomorrow we can still return and ask for more. If
the nationalists aren't able to tell us that this is the
package they want and no more.... The way Cartier
did with MacDonald in 1867. They said we, Quebec,
Lower Canada, we are entering into Confederation if
you give us a federal system with such and such powers for the provinces. Now that agreement lasted
about a hundred years up till, not Duplessis, because
he didn't ask for any new powers, but up till Lesage: it
lasted one hundred years, and I find that respectable.
Let's say one hundred years is too long for the nationalists of today, but if they can't come up with a set of
demands that all of Quebec agrees will last for thirty
years, because in fact they want to come back every
five years or every two years or every month with more
demands, well, yes, in those circumstances I would
prefer a vote on independence. And, you know, we
were supposed to have just that, according to Bill 150,
which called for a vote on independence rather than

on this muddle which they serve up to us as a consensus. But you know very well why we didn't get a vote on independence: it is because Mr. Bourassa would have lost it. The Quebec people would have voted NO to independence because they are sensible; moreover, as you will see, they *will* vote NO.

Paul Maréchal: Good evening, Mr. Trudeau, my name is Paul Maréchal. I noticed in your talk that you seemed very anxious, or at least concerned about the interpretation that the Supreme Court might make of clauses contained in the Charlottetown Agreement. I would like to know first of all if you think the Agreement as it appears, at least the document we have which is not really definitive, is badly drawn, or whether you are afraid of an ever greater control of the judiciary over the legislative process, where it is no longer the government which governs, but rather the Supreme Court which literally governs by virtue of its interpretations.

Mr. Trudeau: I am afraid of neither one nor the other. These questions were discussed ad nauseam between 1787 and 1788 in the 'Federalist Papers' by Madison, Jay and Hamilton. Read above all Essay No. 10, and you will see that men and politicians much more qualified than you and I and those now in power studied these problems thoroughly. And they found that in a federal system, there was a risk that majorities would abuse the rights of minorities, that's the case even in a democracy as lofty as our own. And because they wanted to defend individual rights rather than collective rights, they established a Supreme Court. And it has worked out well.

Mr. Maréchal: Yes but Mr. Trudeau. You know very well that politics is essentially about power relationships between different groups. And you seem to belittle Quebec nationalists, but they are bringing pressures to bear, and it is legitimate for them to do so.

Mr. Trudeau: That's what I replied to Angéline Fournier a while ago. It's legitimate to create pressures. If you don't like a law, you can have it changed; we are all citizens and sometimes we get rid of governments because of the laws they make, and that's fair and square. A law is made to be amended, because it is made for a period of time. Whereas a Constitution, Sir, is not simply a law. Look at the American Constitution which has lasted over two hundred years.

Mr. Maréchal: Do you consider that an ideal model or ...

Mr. Trudeau: You will ask that when ...

Alain Clavet: Your legacy, Mr. Trudeau, is largely the Charter and the equality of official languages. The

Charter and the equality of official languages are in the Charlottetown Agreement. Of course, there are new interpretative clauses for the Canada Clause, which reveal the complexity and the pluralism of contemporary Canadian society, and I can see a balancing mechanism [in the accord]. You conclude automatically that according to you, collective rights will take precedence over individual rights; that remains to be seen. In my opinion we must not underestimate the judges of the Supreme Court. The Charlottetown Accord is definitely not a green light to racism. You like using the word 'reason': I believe it is reasonable to take into account today's Canadian reality, which is pluralist and complex. And it is reasonable moreover to care about the effects of a NO vote on the survival of Canada. It is also reasonable to do things in such a way that Canada works. Canada is going to work some day, and I believe that in a normal country, it is normal to negotiate. What is not normal for a country is to negotiate under the constant threat of the country's disintegration. So, to sum up, my question is that I wonder whether your intellectual position here this evening doesn't fly in the face of your own legacy.

Mr. Trudeau: Well! You tell me about the Charter which is my legacy, and you reassure me by saying that the Charter is in the Consensus of Charlottetown. But the Charter is in the Consensus only in order to say that it does not apply in such and such cases, which is what I have just demonstrated to you. So don't come reassuring me saying the Charter is in there: the Charter is there to the extent that it does not *apply*. I read the articles to you, go re-read my speech. Now you are also telling me about the disintegration of the country, and how it's normal that there should be negotiations. Do you find it normal that people only agree to the Constitution for a few years at a stretch, that if the nationalists aren't happy they will hold a referendum on independence, and if they lose it they will hold another and another until they finally win? Do you find *that* normal?

Mr. Clavet: I believe what is normal is to negotiate in a society as complex as Canada, where in any case Aboriginal people currently live on lands under the Indian Act, lands which are defined on the basis of race as well, and that is a federal law, so there are things to improve in Canada and it's normal to negotiate that. A country in good health, let me continue, a country in good health is a country where people negotiate, without having a knife at their throat. So if the Charlottetown Agreement gives us a negotiating framework in a better climate, that will be good for the economy as well in my opinion. We shouldn't forget the unemployed, we shouldn't forget those people who do not have the means to have abstract positions. Canada has to work. I find that your legacy is the equality of official lnguages and the Charter and a Canada worth saving. So just because we are afraid of some interpretative clauses, of the Canada Clause, is it worthwhile to throw out the baby with the bathwater? So my question is shouldn't we be reasonable?

Mr. Trudeau: Of course, let's be reasonable. You tell me we should negotiate, fine. A Constitution is the result of negotiation, a vision for society as Madame [Fournier] said earlier on. We'll get together, we'll say we want a society on the federal model, where the central government has powers and the provinces have other powers. According to you, how much time should a Constitution last: should we always have to come back and renegotiate, or can we take a breather from time to time?

Mr. Clavet: That's a hypothetical question. What is really happening is that we are negotiating right now and ...

Mr. Trudeau: Yes, and they have negotiated poorly and they are not asking us if we want Canada and Quebec to separate, they are asking us if this is good or rotten negotiation. Well, it's a rotten negotiation. Nobody this evening has shown me a text proving it was good for Canada. Everybody talked to me about the unemployed, and fear about exchange rates, and instability, and so forth. But it seems to me that the current Prime Minister was elected in the name of peace and reconciliation between people and the provinces and the federal government. He has not succeeded, we can understand that. I didn't succeed either, in 1971, and I missed my chance because Mr. Bourassa didn't want the veto in those days. Well, I didn't turn around and say the following day, let's start all over again: no, we missed our chance, so we let it drop, held an election and then left it to someone else to try another time. He [Mr. Mulroney] failed with Meech Lake, so why did he try all over again when it wasn't working? He started again *because he saw he was going to lose his friend Lucien Bouchard if he didn't start up again*, and he would lose others unless he offered a distinct society to Quebec nationalists. So he started all over again, and it's he who has created instability and unemployment. Was I the one, or was it you, or was it the government that tried again, after screwing up, and in fact screwed up again? To serve this document up to us, and tell us if we don't accept it the country would go into self-destruct. 'Well yeah', they say, 'you're destroying the country', 'well vote for me' and we'll all elect Mr. Mulroney again because after all he got us this great consensus, that's what they're after. You're telling me we have to support *that* in order to have stability. OK. Let's elect Mr. Mulroney and we'll have stability: that no doubt is your conclusion.

Mr. Daniel Schecter: Hello, my name is Daniel Schecter, and I am a CEGEP student and the son of

Stephen Schecter who writes for *Cité libre*. My father couldn't be with us tonight, so he asked me: 'Dear readers, to remind you that we are living in a post-modern society, and therefore we have to consider that the Charlottetown Accord gives Canada the first post-modern Constitution in the world. For once Canada is in the avant-garde, and this is no time to say NO.

As people ought to know by now,' says my father, 'post-modern society is characterized by a multiplicity of groups asserting their rights. This may be regrettable, but that's the way it is, and unless the Canadian people...'

Mr. Trudeau: This may be regrettable, is that what you are saying?

Mr. Schecter: Yes, that's right. '...And unless the Canadian people...'

Mr. Trudeau: Listen, send me the letter, I don't have the intention, please send me the letter, I am quite capable of reading it.

Mr. Schecter: Sorry. '...This may be regrettable, but that's the way it is, and unless the Canadian people are ready to reelect Mr. Trudeau, or in your place my father, it is hard to imagine how a new round of talks will lead to an accord substantially different from the Charlottetown Accord. For this reason, and for several others which I cannot elaborate upon as well as my father, I would therefore like ...'

Mr. Tombs: We don't have much time. We'll cut it right there. We'll move on to the ...

Mr. Trudeau: Besides, there's no point in your reading me a speech...

Mr. Schecter: 'I call upon you, dear readers...'

Mr. Tombs: We'll cut in right there. Yes, a question over here.

Patrick Gagnon: My name is Patrick Gagnon and my question will be brief. Mr. Trudeau, to be frank, for the first time in a long time, we have the unanimous agreement of the provinces, and First Ministers. I have to tell you that there are quite a few people here tonight who will support the YES side and we will be doing so for the simple reason that we believe there is a lot to be gained from the Canadian experience. And the conclusion, or rather the continuation - but I wouldn't want to quote General De Gaulle, Mr. Trudeau, but I should say to you the way he did to the crowd in Paris in 1968 that 'our country, my fellow citizens of France, is at the edge of the abyss'.

Mr. Trudeau: [in English] *Next!*

Michel Sarra-Bournet: Mr. Trudeau, you mentioned The Federalist Papers. According to the theory of federalism, the two levels of government are meant to balance each other, pulling one one way, and the other the other way. And at present, we seem to be fighting both governments at the same time, and I find it takes a certain degree of courage to go against both governments at present. Having said that, I find just as you do that this agreement is full of contradictions, and that it is an agreement without a national vision. But in my opinion, it is without national *visions*, in the plural, because I believe we have two nations. What I wanted to say is finally that the notion of collective rights, for me, is a necessary one, and they aren't incompatible with individual rights. And in fact, without collective rights there would be no Canadian state. Your Canadian state, Mr. Trudeau, would not exist, because the Canadian state acts in the name of the Canadian collectivity, just as the National Assembly of Quebec acts in the name of a collectivity when it legislates to give rights to the anglophones of Quebec, or when it legislates to pass motions to recognize the Aboriginal peoples of Quebec as nations as well as the treaties of government. So it isn't the *tyranny* of the-French-Canadian majority of Quebec expressing itself by means of the collective rights of the Quebec state. Finally, my question has to do with your Charter of Rights which offers us a very broad notion of fundamental freedoms. According to Senator Michael Kirby, you have insisted on making linguistic rights fundamental freedoms; you have presented that to us as a freedom, a fundamental individual right. And then, in fact, Mr. Kirby said that your objective, and that of the Charter of Rights, was to attack Bill 101 in Quebec. I would like you to explain why, in 1982, you accepted that the notwithstanding clause be applicable to freedom of expression but not to linguistic rights.

Mr. Trudeau: You speak of collective rights, and the previous question mentioned collective rights, as if they were of no importance. Collective rights *are* important: what we need is to determine whether they will take precedence over individual rights, that's all. So people have said, 'it's not as upsetting as all that, the judges aren't stupid, they will know what to do with collective rights! Mr. Bourassa has said, word for word, 'I am the only premier who has dared trample individual rights in the name of collective rights'. I don't have to draw you a picture: it was Bill 178. He took rights away from people who had been told by the courts they had the right to put up signs in small letters in English. Mr. Bourassa passed a law saying 'Inside but not outside'. That's what collective rights are about. And it's the unhappy result of collective rights running into each other. You are quite right that Canada is a collectivity. It's a nation, the Canadian nation, Quebec is a collectivity, it's the Quebec collectivity.

And if collective rights must predominate, then certainly the greater will predominate over the smaller.

Does that mean that in Canada, and it was true during a good part of our history, that English Canada could largely ignore the rights of francophones. And if the collective rights of Quebec predominate, then that means [Quebec] can pretty much ignore the Aboriginal peoples, who say that if Quebec separated, they would not necessarily join Quebec. Which Quebec does not appreciate. And that is why the theory of collective rights is a dangerous one. Larger and smaller collectivities confront each other in the heart of one and the same country, and that can lead eventually to civil wars. That's what collective rights are all about. And that's why the French Revolution established liberty as a fundamental right. No-one is subject in his fundamental rights to the state: that is *liberalism* - which says the individual in the exercise of his fundamental rights precedes the state, and all individuals are equal - that's the American Constitution, that's the Universal Declaration of Human Rights. So I'm not against collective rights. My family is a collectivity, we at *Cité libre* are a collectivity with majorities and minorities. It's plain for all to see. But the question is not whether collectivities are legitimate: they exist, I am not denying that. I am asking whether it is better for collective rights of the majority to be able to abolish the collective rights of a minority. If the answer is yes, the minority will say 'But we too form a collectivity, so we will separate from the majority and make our own state'. That's what is happening in Bosnia. Everyone will have their own little state, and minorities will be badly treated, so the minorities will say they're leaving. It's the whole problem of Canada, and the problem I wanted to put an end to in adopting the Charter of Rights and Freedoms, in saying listen, citizens, you are all first of all *equal among yourselves*, and that your rights take priority over those of the state. That doesn't mean that the state is not a collectivity or doesn't have rights: of *course* it has rights, it has the right, according to our Constitution, to make laws. The citizen pays his taxes, and obeys the law. So the collectivity has rights. It's just that according to my philosophy, according to liberal philosophy and the philosophy of the Enlightenment, the collectivity always has rights delegated to it by the individual. The collectivity is not the *bearer* of rights: it *receives* the rights it exercises from the citizens.

Mr. Tombs: I know there are still a lot of questions out there. But we have to move on to the press conference. So let's all thank Mr. Trudeau for speaking to us this evening.

PRESS CONFERENCE

Mr. Guy Sarault acts as moderator of the conference

Mr. Guy Sarault: As I said just now, questions are going to be asked one by one, French, English, network after network.

Welcome to the press conference, ladies and gentlemen. We are going to start with Madame Francine Bastien of Radio-Canada, please.

Mme. Bastien: Mr. Trudeau, once again you have shaken the hopes of Quebec nationalists, and it's hard to make head or tail of your recommendation to the people to vote NO, without serving the interests of Quebec nationalists.

Mr. Trudeau: I didn't particularly slam Quebec nationalists. It seems to me I demonstrated this evening the misery of Canadian politics, if you like, in general, that of all the politicians who wrote this agreement. I feel it is full of errors and weakens Canada.

But if you are the least bit informed, you know that Mr. Parizeau does not have the same reasons I do for saying NO. Mr. Parizeau is saying NO because he feels Quebec should go and become independent: and this agreement does not lead directly to independence, there remain other steps. I am against it because I find it weakens Canada too much, and Canada has become altogether too provincialized. Canada is already the most decentralized country in the world, of all the countries of the OECD, which means of all the industrialized countries. Canada, then, is the most decentralized, and here they come with a further massive decentralization of power which is offered to us along with an increase in the presence of the provinces in both the Canadian Government and Parliament.

Mme. Bastien: There are different types of NO, Mr. Trudeau, that is what you are saying. Will there then be different types of NO when the time comes to count the votes?

Mr. Trudeau: Isn't it obvious to you that some people like me will vote NO because they are against independence, and others will vote NO because they are for independence? But do you think that is any reason to fall into a trap? Should Mr. Parizeau vote YES because Mr. Trudeau is voting NO? Perhaps you should ask Mr. Parizeau to change his mind because if he is associated with me, people will say: Mr. Parizeau you are helping the Trudeau side. Go talk to him about that.

Mr. Sarault: Neil MacDonald, CBC.

Mr. MacDonald: Mr. Trudeau, your own former Quebec lieutenant, Mr. Lalonde, said this week that while he might admire your intellectual analysis, he's voting YES like Mr. Chrétien because the world of politics is is one of compromise. I was wondering how you might respond to that assertion, that realpolitik dictates a YES vote.

Mr. Trudeau: Well, politicians have to make tactical decisions and for reasons which good analysts could explain to you it's a difficult thing for a politician, a federalist politician, like Mr. Chrétien, to associate himself with Mr. Parizeau. And because the YES, the YES proponents are muddleing the question and we're being told that a NO vote means a NO to Canada and when that's been told, when that's been said by the Prime Minister and by the Federal Cabinet and by the Provincial Cabinet and by the bankers and by the business men, you can't blame the people for wondering what they're to do. But me, I don't have to be concerned about that, I'm not in politics any more. I look at this Accord, I see it as a weakening, a crippling of Canada, and I say I will vote against it. If some other people are dishonest enough to say: Ah! therefore he's helping separatism, you know, that's their problem, it's not mine, and it's a dishonest interpretation of the vote. And I believe that if you look across Canada, you will see a lot of NO votes which are not Mr. Manning's and which are not the separatists'. If Canadians are free people, and I think they are, and if they can read the project of the Constitution and I think they can, if we put it in their hands, I think they will see that it is a crippling blow to the Canada that we know and love and therefore the only answer to a crippling blow is to say I'm not in agreement with it. It doesn't mean that you're voting like Mr. Parizeau, it means you're voting like a *Canadian*.

Mr. MacDonald: At the end of the day, is there a difference between one NO and another?

Mr. Trudeau: It's in the eye of the beholder. If you think my vote is the same as Mr. Parizeau's, well you're a peculiar form of analyst.

Mr. Sarault: Mr. Alain Gravel, TVA, please.

Alain Gravel: Mr. Trudeau, what do you reply to people, to the YES side, who imply that a NO in this referendum is one step towards the independence of Quebec? How do you reply to them?

Mr. Trudeau: Well, I reply that they are greatly mistaken, because the referendum question is not YES or NO to the independence of Quebec, the referendum question is YES or NO to this constitutional package. So if the question is honest, you have to be completely honest in the way you express your answer. If the question is really a YES or NO vote for this constitutional package, then a NO vote means no to this constitutional package, and not no to Canada.

Mr. Gravel: Aren't you afraid that...

Mr. Trudeau: Sure I'm afraid: that journalists don't do their job properly, and that they make everyone believe that the YES side is the side of those who love Canada, and the NO side is the side of people who don't love Canada. I will say my truth; you say yours.

Mr. Sarault: Alan Fryer, CTV.

Mr. Fryer: Mr. Trudeau, how do you respond to criticism about Premier Bourassa among others that yours is the voice from the past, that you're out of touch with the political realities in Quebec today?

Mr. Trudeau: Well, Pythagoras is a man from the past, but two and two are still four.

Mr. Sarault: Mr. Denis Leduc, Quatre-Saisons... Go ahead Mr. Vastel, he isn't here.

Michel Vastel, Edimédia: Do you believe you are weakening or you are undermining the leadership of Mr. Chrétien, a little like the way you did with Mr.

Turner, by taking a position that divides the party you were leader of?

Mr. Trudeau: Not at all. I'm not the one to divide the Party; those who come up with the same conclusions as me will vote NO. Those who come up with the same conclusions as Mr. Chrétien will vote YES. I respect Mr. Chrétien, I talk to him, he is a friend, and I want, I hope he will be the next Prime Minister. But I know he is a man who has to take tactical decisions and I respect them and I think he must respect my own.

Mr. Vastel: And you accept that the head of the Party, for tactical reasons, as you say - well, it could have been you...

Mr. Trudeau: Good Lord, it *was* me, it was me, I made tactical decisions when I accepted the notwithstanding clause in order to get a Charter of Rights. It was either *no* Charter or a slightly weakened Charter, and I preferred taking a tactical decision right away. Mr. Chrétien has the right to take such decisions as well.

Mr. Sarault: Peter Maser, Southam.

Mr. Maser: Mr. Trudeau, if as you say this agreement deal is a crippling blow to the Canada we know and love, can we expect to hear from you in coming weeks, expect to see you take this message that you have to other forums, other parts of Canada?

Mr. Trudeau: I think with these twenty microphones here and all these cameras, I will have been heard loud and clear, I don't see any need to speak anymore. But you never know.

Mr. Sarault: Roland Parent, Presse Canadienne: no question? Lysiane Gagnon, La Presse, no question? Robert De Serres, Radio Mutuel.

Mr. De Serres: Yes, Mr. Trudeau, by taking a firm position in favour of NO this evening during your talk for pretty well the same reasons as Mr. Bouchard and Parizeau, you are confusing Quebeckers....

Mr. Trudeau: No, no, *you* are confusing things. You have listened to my reasons, so saying I am for a NO for the same reasons as *them* is to misunderstand. They say NO because they want a weaker Canada. I say NO because I want a stronger Canada. So don't go saying it's for the same reasons.

Mr. De Serres: With the same arguments but not for the same reasons, you are confusing Quebeckers. What can you say to Quebeckers so it will be clear?

Mr. Trudeau: Well, I repeat what I said earlier on. Canada is already the most decentralized country in the world, and if Quebec, which from the point of view of revenue is below-average, wants to continue receiving equalization payments, which is well and good, if Quebeckers want to belong to a large and wonderful country, if they want to be at home everywhere in Canada and travel with a Canadian passport, if they want to be proud to be Canadian, they should vote NO. But if it's just in order to weaken Canada, the way Mr. Parizeau wants and this [Canada] clause wants, I suggest they explain that their NO is not a YES to independence, and that they correct journalists and politicians who would have people believe that a NO is a YES to independence. Because the question, you see, is 'do you want this Accord or not?'. It isn't 'do you want Quebec independence or not?'; it is 'do you want this Accord?'. And this Accord is bad for Canada. Canada is already the most decentralized of all industrialized countries in the world. So its to become even more decentralized? With this Accord it is doubtful that we can continue to have new shared-cost programmes like health insurance. That's what's *great* about Canada: everybody shares. The rich provinces help the poor ones, the rich taxpayers help the poor taxpayers. That's what Canada is, and if we want to live in a country of brotherhood, we shouldn't weaken the heart and the brain and the nervous system of the country.

Mike Duffy, CTV: Mr. Trudeau, in the face of the millions of dollars to be spent by the federal government and the YES committee to sell this deal, isn't there almost a sacred duty on your part as a privy councillor, if you feel as you said a moment ago, to carry your message extensively from now until the 26th of October?

Mr. Trudeau: Well, I'm relying on *you*, Mike, to carry my message. That's what your job is all about, you've been doing it for years, you've been doing it very well. Carry on!

Mr. Duffy: Supplementary. Iona Campagnolo scoffed today at those who suggest that they need to see the legal text before they can make a real judgment. She says we don't need to see our own house insurance policy, so why do we need to see the text of this Accord?

Mr. Trudeau: Because when she doesn't look at her house insurance policy, she makes sure her lawyer looks at it. Now, I'm her lawyer, and I looked at it for her, and I tell her she should vote NO.

Mr. Graham Fraser: Mr. Trudeau, you made a distinction between questions of principle and questions of tactics. I was wondering if you can tell us what you see as the tactical consequence of the NO vote that you recommend?

Mr. Trudeau: I think that if it were to carry substantially in other provinces and in Quebec, I think it would shake up the politicians a little bit, it would make them realize they can't with bombast and bluster frighten Canadians to vote YES when they think they should vote NO. And maybe we're going to change the politicians and maybe there'll be more respect for the Canadian people. Or they'll ask the right questions. Maybe that is another solution. You know we were supposed to have a referendum from Mr. Bourassa 'Do you want sovereignty or not'. He did not ask it. Why? Because when you *ask* the question, you have to vote for the YES, and he didn't want to campaign for sovereignty, because he knew he would have lost. The Quebec people don't *want* independence. It's the political leaders who want more power for themselves. As I said upstairs, the way the exercise the powers they *have* leaves a lot to be desired. Many of the problems we have can be solved by laws, not by changing the Constitution. When you change the Constitution, it's for a long time, and we know that Mr. Bourassa has already said this is only a stage in his demands, he's telling the Quebec people that if they vote YES, it's a YES to this particular deal but that doesn't preclude them from asking for more tomorrow. And he said that we've still got the right to self-determination in our party's Constitution. So we'll be around tomorrow and ask for more. That's why I'm saying: if Canadians want peace, they should say NO to the politicians. We want the status quo, we want to work with it. So go get yourself elected again, then maybe we'll listen to you, but right now you have lost your credibility, you're trying to scare us into voting YES to a Constitution that is bad for Canada, and we don't scare easily.

Mr. Sarault: Mme. Lysiane Gagnon, La Presse.

Mme. Gagnon: Mr. Trudeau, it may come as some surprise to Quebeckers to hear you always blaming Quebec for everything that happens. It's true that Quebec had a lot of demands etc. But finally in this round, called 'the Canada round', haven't other provinces such as Alberta asked for and obtained a lot? So why, when for example with Senate reform, which neither Quebec nor Quebeckers ever asked for, why are you always making Quebec your target, Quebec nationalism, while the nationalism of the Aboriginal peoples is doing very nicely, indeed, and the appetites of Newfoundland and the western provinces, for example, are voracious?

Mr. Trudeau: Just understand that where you speak of Quebec, I am speaking of Quebecois nationalists, in other words, the leaders who want to have more power for themselves. The crutch which the dis-

tinct society represents is nothing more than an avo-
wal of weakness by some of the nationalist leaders. As
for me, I believe that French Canadians, man for man,
can stand up for themselves and compete with
anyone. Earlier on during my talk, I also named the
Aboriginal peoples, and I said they were out of line
with their collective rights. And I named other provinces asking for changes to the Senate and wanting to
get the most powers possible for themselves. And I
even explained that it's in the nature of a provincial
politician always to want more power for his province.
And I know, and you know as well, that it was Quebec
nationalists, starting with those who influenced Lesage, who opened up the constitutional file. When Mr.
Robarts convened a Constitutional Conference in
1967, it was at the request of Mr. Daniel Johnson: it
wasn't Mr. Robarts, who would probably have been
able to put up with the Constitution. So we should recognize this and I think it is a historic fact that this
round of demands started with Quebec. All the provinces coming to the table wanted to profit from that.
And I have often denounced, and you have heard me
do so, all ten Premiers, including Mr. Levesque at the
time, who presented to the federal government the
Château Consensus. Because each one of them, to use
a delicious expression you have already used yourself,
each provincial politician said 'the buffet is open, and
Trudeau is dishing things out, so let's go get something'. Well, the difficulty you see, is that I didn't want

to give anything more up, I told them 'you are asking too much, you are in the process of destroying the country', and that is what's happening now. Quebec opened the round, and I think that if unfortunately this consensus were approved and became the Constitution, it won't be Ontario opening the ball next time, in any case, they haven't said so. Whereas Mr. Bourassa has said he will do so. He said that a YES is not irreversible, and that after a YES, Quebec will still have the right to self-determination and there will be other demands. So, I could avoid naming him, to avoid offending Quebeckers here, but what do you want? We have to recognize the hard facts and the truth, whatever it may be.

Mr. Jeffrey Simpson: You spoke tonight about the Charter and its effect on aboriginal rights. Do you favour aboriginal self-government, that that particular matter could be resolved. And secondly, as a supplementary to Graham Fraser's queston, do you think if there's a NO vote, there should be a constitutional moratorium for a certain period of time, such as Mr. Manning has proposed in Alberta?

Mr. Trudeau: The answer to both questions is Yes. On the second one, it's obvious that if there is a NO vote, there has to be a moratorium, because if there's a NO vote, Mr. Mulroney will have lost his credibility, if he's got any left, and Mr. Bourassa will have lost it too. So there'll have to be a moratorium, they'll have to talk about something else, and hopefully, they'll have to go in to an election within a year or so. And therefore it's in their interest rather than to brag about the fact that Canada said NO to them, they'll probably forget about the Constitution for a little while, which will be a great relief to us all. Now, on my Yes to 'do I favour aboriginal self-government', not only do I favour it, but I *proposed it* first in a White Paper back in 1969 when I proposed the abolition of the Indian Act. But the Indians were not ready for it. They said no, no, no, not yet, give us time. They were psyched out. And in the 80s, I introduced a bill in the House of Commons, my government did, which precisely offered self-government to the native people, to those who wanted to exercise it and even to the Métis. So that's, you know, that's old hat. Difference is, we put it in a law, and it's a law which was taken up by those Indian tribes who wanted to take it up. But it is wrong to put it in the Constitution until we work out the quirks, to put it into the Constitution, with this kind of vague project about a third order of government without explaining it to us. We are not talking here about a municipal government, this is a *third order* of government with legislatures and other levels ofgovernments. And you know, maybe it's a good move, but we'd like to know, *we'd like to see the legal text*. But the government seems to think like Mrs. Campagnolo that nobody reads legal texts. Well, you know, I've been reading the Constitution all my life. I taught it, I even meddled in it a bit, and muddled things up. I was talking to John Polanyi the other day, the Nobel Prize winner, and I was saying, 'well, what duty does a scientist have in telling the politicians about the dangers of nuclear war or chemical warfare and so on'. 'Well', he says, 'he shouldn't act like a politician'. I hope John doesn't think I'm misquoting him, but he says it's our duty as scientists to show the danger signals. Well, I think it's *my* duty as a former professor of constitutional law to point out the danger signals. The press can do what they want with it, the Canadian people can do what they want with it. But you know I think I would be remiss in my duty as a Canadian and as an ex-professor of constitutional law, I would be remiss if I didn't point out to Canadians that this is a very bad deal for the Canada that we know. There will be another Canada after, if this passes, but it will be a weakened and crippled Canada and it won't be a Canada of sharing because we will have gotten rid of all the economic tools that permit us to share.

Mr. Sarault: So, a last question for Mr. Michel Auger, for the readers of Le Journal de Montreal.

Mr. Auger: I would like to know how the compromises resulting from the Charlottetown Accord of today are less acceptable than the compromises you were induced to make, the compromises you offered in 1981.

Mr. Trudeau: Well, in '81 we managed to repatriate the Constitution of Canada, which was something all federal governments since 1927 had tried to do and failed. I could have said, a hundred fourteen years after the birth of Canada, I could have said we are the only country in the world which cannot have and amend its own Constitution on its territory, the only independent country in the world in this position. Or I could have listened to the Supreme Court tell us: 'here is the Law, here is what the Law, the Constitution and convention will allow you to do to amend, to repatriate the Constitution', I listened to the Supreme Court. But in order to obtain the consent of a substantial number of provinces, I was obliged to make some compromises. In return, I obtained the Charter or Rights and Freedoms, in return I obtained an amending formula. And what did the provinces obtain? Well, a few improvements in the area of natural resources, that's not bad, that's an exchange. So you are asking me why I made compromises: it's because I got something in exchange, something that nobody had achieved since 1867. Finally, we did it, and I was obliged to make a small compromise. Now you are asking me what the federal government, what do Canadians as Canadians and not just citizens of their provinces obtain in this Charter [the Charlottetown

Accord]? Do you have an answer? Zero, zero, they get nothing.

Mr. Auger: Quebec's [participation] would have made it legitimate.

Mr. Trudeau: Legitimacy for Quebec? *But there's no lack of legitimacy.* The Supreme Court, at the express request of Quebec in an action initiated by Quebec, the Supreme Court said Quebec was included in the Constitution. Everybody knows Mr. Levesque tried to block the repatriation and that he formed an alliance with seven other provinces to block the repatriation. But at some point he got tangled up in his skates, and he broke up the Gang of Eight, and so the others said Levesque is letting us drop, so they let him drop. Mr. Levesque came down to earth again, and I repatriated the Constitution for Quebec and for all of Canada. And what's more, is that I was approved by 96% of Quebec Members of Parliament, and something like 35% of Quebec deputies in the National Assembly. Which comes out to a weighted total of all Quebec deputies of 65% in favour of the Act to repatriate the Constitution of 1982. It's hard to say Quebec got the brush-off when 65% of its deputies voted in favour. Of course, for people who want to rewrite history and who talk of the night of the long knives and have invented a whole mythology, it's easy to do things like that if we don't let ourselves be encumbered by the truth. Voilà.

Not yet a subcriber to

Cité libre ?

What are you waiting for ?

Please enter my subscription to Cité Libre.
Enclosed please find my cheque payable to
PERIODICA (Box 444, Outremont, QC H2V 4R6)
in the amount of 32,10 $ (Canada), or 38,00 $ (foreign),
for 10 numbers.
Or I wish to pay by ☐ VISA , ☐ MASTERCARD,
or ☐ DEBIT CARD :

Card number .... exp. ....

Signature ....

Name ....

Address...

City ....

Province/Country............................ Postal Code ....

 ACHEVÉ   D'IMPRIMER
EN   OCTOBRE   **1992**
SUR LES PRESSES DE
PAYETTE & SIMMS INC.
À SAINT-LAMBERT, P.Q.